It Is Windy

Kelly Doudna

Consulting Editor Monica Marx, M.A./Reading Specialist

Published by SandCastle™, an imprint of ABDO Publishing Company, 4940 Viking Drive, Edina, Minnesota 55435.

Printed in the United States.

Credits
Edited by: Pam Price
Curriculum Coordinator: Nancy Tuminelly
Cover and Interior Design and Production: Mighty Media
Photo Credits: Corbis Images, Digital Vision, Eyewire Images, PhotoDisc, Stockbyte

Library of Congress Cataloging-in-Publication Data

Doudna, Kelly, 1963-
    It is windy / Kelly Doudna.
        p. cm. -- (The weather)
    Includes index.
    Summary: A very simple introduction to the characteristics of wind.
    ISBN 1-57765-778-0
    1. Winds--Juvenile literature. [1. Winds.] I. Title.

QC931.4 .D68 2002
551.51'8--dc21

                                                                    2002018370

SandCastle™ books are created by a professional team of educators, reading specialists, and content developers around five essential components that include phonemic awareness, phonics, vocabulary, text comprehension, and fluency. All books are written, reviewed, and leveled for guided reading, early intervention reading, and Accelerated Reader® programs and designed for use in shared, guided, and independent reading and writing activities to support a balanced approach to literacy instruction.

Let Us Know

After reading the book, SandCastle would like you to tell us your stories about reading. What is your favorite page? Was there something hard that you needed help with? Share the ups and downs of learning to read. We want to hear from you! To get posted on the ABDO Publishing Company Web site, send us email at:

sandcastle@abdopub.com

SandCastle Level: Beginning

What is the wind?

Wind is moving air.

Gentle wind is a
breeze.

Strong wind is a gale.

Wind turns windmills.

Wind shapes sand into dunes.

Wind carries seeds
through the air.

Wind blows bubbles
from Ann's wand.

Wind spins Kim's pinwheel.

John likes to fly his kite on a windy day.

Do you?

Picture Index

bubbles, p. 17

seeds, p. 15

dunes, p. 13

windmills, p. 11

kite, p. 21

Match the words to the pictures

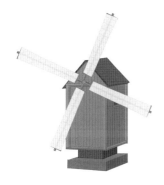 

bubbles   seeds

kite   windmill

23

About SandCastle™

A professional team of educators, reading specialists, and content developers created the SandCastle™ series to support young readers as they develop reading skills and strategies and increase their general knowledge. The SandCastle™ series has four levels that correspond to early literacy development in young children. The levels are provided to help teachers and parents select the appropriate books for young readers.

Emerging Readers
(no flags)

Beginning Readers
(1 flag)

Transitional Readers
(2 flags)

Fluent Readers
(3 flags)

These levels are meant only as a guide. All levels are subject to change.

To see a complete list of SandCastle™ books and other nonfiction titles from ABDO Publishing Company, visit **www.abdopub.com** or contact us at:

4940 Viking Drive, Edina, Minnesota 55435 • 1-800-800-1312 • fax: 1-952-831-1632